Eternal Love

Alexis. H

 pencil

ISBN 978-93-5667-954-2
© Alexis. H 2023

Published in India 2023 by Pencil

A brand of
One Point Six Technologies Pvt. Ltd.
Unit no. 26, Ground Floor, Building A1,
Wadala Truck Terminal Road,
Near Post Office, Antop Hill, Mumbai - 400037
E connect@thepencilapp.com
W www.thepencilapp.com

Author biography

Hi everyone, My name is Alexis Hagins and I am 21 years old. I currently don't have a profession but my big dream is to become a chef and open my own restaurant one day. I wanted to write a story that would be enchanting and magical for all readers and that would take them on a journey to a whole new world in their imagination. I hope you all enjoy this book and I hope it brings you joy and happiness.

CONTENTS

Chapter 1 Lost in the Labyrinth 6

Chapter 2 The Enigmatic Guide 9

Chapter 3 The Silver Forest's Enchantment 12

Chapter 4 Love's Resonance 15

Chapter 5 Triumph of Light.. 18

Chapter 6 A New Dawn 21

Chapter 7 The Legacy of Eternal Love 24

Chapter 8 An Everlasting Flame 27

Chapter 9 The Celestial Union 30

Chapter 10 The Eternal Flame Rekindled 33

Chapter 11 The Return of the Beloved 36

Chapter 12 The Everlasting Legacy 40

Chapter 13 The Cosmic Reunion.. 43

Chapter 14 The Tapestry of Love.. 47

Chapter 15 The Celestial Symphony..................................... 51

Chapter 16 The Infinite Tapestry.. 54

Chapter 17 The Essence Within... 57

Chapter 18 The Dance of Connection 60

Chapter 19 The Awakening of Compassion....................... 63

Chapter 20 The Eternal Legacy of Love............................. 66

Chapter 1 Lost in the Labyrinth

The crisp morning air clung to Jewel's skin as she stepped out onto the bustling streets of Earth. A planet so foreign to her, it seemed like a distant dream. She had been forced to leave her own world, her people, everything she held dear, behind. Now, her days were spent navigating the complexities of this new existence, trying to make it through the mundane routine that had become her life.

Jewel, with her luminous azure eyes and radiant silver hair, possessed an ethereal beauty that captivated those around her. She had been chosen, an emissary of her people, to come to Earth in search of hope, a way to save her beloved home from the impending darkness that threatened to consume it. The fate of her world rested on her slender shoulders, and she carried the weight with determination and unwavering resilience.

With each passing day, Jewel's heart yearned for her family, her friends, and the familiar comforts of her homeland. Memories of laughter, love, and the vibrant hues of her people's luminous energy haunted her thoughts, reminding her of what was at stake. She clung to the hope of being reunited with them, to bring salvation and restore the balance that had been shattered.

However, the path ahead was treacherous, for there were forces at play that sought to hinder Jewel's quest. In the shadows, a nameless darkness lurked, its tendrils reaching out, threatening to suffocate any glimmer of light that Jewel carried within her. She felt the weight of its presence, an ever-present reminder that her journey would be fraught with peril and opposition.

As Jewel made her way through the bustling city, she observed the inhabitants of this foreign land. They scurried about their lives, their faces etched with worry, yet unaware of the imminent danger looming over them all. For it was not just her own people that Jewel sought to save but also the people of Earth, unwitting pawns in a greater cosmic battle.

She had heard whispers of a hidden prophecy, one that spoke of an eternal love that could unlock the key to vanquishing the encroaching darkness. It was a love that transcended boundaries, a love that had the power to heal and illuminate even the darkest corners of existence. Jewel knew deep in her heart that she carried this love within her, but she also knew that she had yet to discover its true magnitude.

With every sunrise and sunset, Jewel pressed forward, her determination unyielding. She sought guidance from the ancient texts that had been entrusted to her, deciphering their cryptic messages in hopes of unraveling the secrets they held. Each word, each symbol held the promise of salvation and the hope of reuniting with her family.

But time was not her ally. The forces of darkness were growing stronger, their reach extending further with each passing day. Jewel felt the weight of urgency pressing against her, urging her to quicken her pace, to unlock the mysteries that held the answers she so desperately sought.

As Jewel walked, she couldn't shake the feeling of being watched. She cast wary glances over her shoulder, sensing eyes upon her, unseen and menacing. The whispers in the wind spoke of ancient prophecies, of the chosen one who would bring about the triumph of light over darkness. She knew her path would be riddled with tests and tribulations, but she was prepared to face them head-on.

For she was Jewel, a beacon of hope in the face of despair, a warrior of light on a mission to restore balance to the universe. With each step, she wove her destiny, determined to overcome the darkness that threatened to consume her world.

Chapter 2 The Enigmatic Guide

Jewel's quest to save her world and the people of Earth had brought her to the heart of a bustling city. The towering skyscrapers loomed above her, casting long shadows that seemed to mirror the darkness that plagued her thoughts. She knew that time was of the essence, and she sought guidance from a mysterious figure who was said to possess the knowledge she needed.

As Jewel ventured deeper into the city's labyrinthine streets, she couldn't help but feel a sense of unease. The buildings seemed to press in on her, their cold facades indifferent to the struggles that weighed heavily on her heart. Her senses heightened, she sought the subtle signs that would lead her to the enigmatic guide.

At last, Jewel arrived at a humble storefront nestled amidst the grandeur of the cityscape. The sign above the door simply read, "The Oracle's Haven." Her heart quickened with a mix of anticipation and trepidation as she pushed open the creaking wooden door, the bell chiming softly.

The interior of the Haven was dimly lit, its walls adorned with ancient tapestries and shelves lined with weathered books. The air carried the scent of aged parchment and incense, infusing the space with an otherworldly aura. Jewel's eyes were drawn to a figure seated at a wooden desk, their face concealed beneath a hooded cloak.

Approaching cautiously, Jewel spoke, her voice trembling with a mixture of hope and uncertainty, "Are you the Oracle? The one who can guide me on my journey?"

The figure nodded, their voice gentle yet carrying an air of wisdom. "I am but a vessel, a conduit for the cosmic knowledge that seeks to aid those in need. What brings you to seek my guidance, child?"

Jewel found solace in the Oracle's soothing words, feeling an inexplicable connection to the being before her. She recounted the plight of her people, the impending darkness, and her quest to find the eternal love that could save them all. The Oracle listened intently, their eyes seeming to see beyond the physical realm.

After a moment of silence, the Oracle raised a hand, palm up, and a soft glow emanated from their fingers. In the air above their hand, a holographic image formed—a map of celestial constellations and intricate symbols intertwined.

"This is the Path of Illumination," the Oracle explained. "To find the eternal love you seek, you must embark on a journey that will test your strength, faith, and resolve. The stars will be your guide, but you must decipher the hidden meanings within."

Jewel's gaze locked onto the mesmerizing display, her heart brimming with renewed hope. She knew that this journey would be no ordinary one, but she was ready to face any challenge that lay ahead.

The Oracle continued, "Seek the Heartstone—a sacred relic said to hold the essence of eternal love. It is guarded in the realm of the Silver Forest, where shadows dance and illusions abound. There, you will face trials that will test your perception, for darkness seeks to deceive."

Jewel nodded, absorbing the Oracle's words, committing them to memory. She knew that the path ahead would be perilous, but she was determined to overcome every obstacle and rescue her people from the encroaching darkness.

As she prepared to leave, the Oracle placed a small, intricately carved box on the desk before her. "This gift holds a fragment of the eternal love you seek," they whispered. "Guard it well, for it will be a beacon of hope in your darkest moments."

With gratitude, Jewel accepted the box, holding it close to her heart. She felt a surge of warmth, a flicker of the love that burned brightly.

Chapter 3 The Silver Forest's Enchantment

Armed with the guidance of the Oracle and the precious fragment of eternal love, Jewel embarked on her journey to the fabled realm of the Silver Forest. The path that lay before her was shrouded in mystery and danger, but she pressed forward, fueled by a steadfast determination to fulfill her mission.

The Silver Forest stood as an enigmatic realm, whispered about in ancient tales passed down through generations. Legends spoke of its ethereal beauty, with trees adorned in silver leaves that shimmered like moonlight. Yet, behind its captivating facade, the forest held secrets, illusions, and challenges that would test Jewel's resolve.

As she stepped into the forest's threshold, a hushed silence enveloped her. The air carried an otherworldly stillness, broken only by the soft rustling of leaves underfoot. The path ahead meandered through a labyrinth of ancient trees, their branches reaching out like skeletal fingers.

Navigating through the ethereal maze, Jewel relied on her intuition, seeking signs and symbols that might guide her. The silver glow that bathed the forest provided an eerie luminescence, casting elongated shadows that danced among the trees.

As Jewel ventured deeper, the forest's enchantments began to manifest. Illusions flickered at the edges of her vision, beckoning her off the path and into the realm of deception. She recognized these trials as the darkness attempting to thwart her mission, but she remained steadfast, focused on her goal.

The forest seemed to shift and morph around her, presenting challenges designed to confuse and confound. A mirrored lake reflected a distorted image of Jewel, enticing her to question her identity and purpose. She gazed into her own eyes, searching for the unwavering light within, and reminded herself of the love that burned within her soul.

Pressing onward, Jewel encountered a bridge made of intertwining thorns, their sharp edges poised to ensnare and deter. With caution and determination, she navigated the treacherous path, her resolve unyielding. Each step forward brought her closer to the heart of the forest, closer to the answers she sought.

Amidst the forest's whispering shadows, Jewel stumbled upon an ancient, weathered stone pedestal. Nestled upon it, bathed in silver light, was the Heartstone—the sacred relic said to contain the essence of eternal love. Jewel's heart swelled with anticipation as she approached, her hands trembling as she reached out to touch the stone.

As her fingertips brushed against its cool surface, a surge of energy coursed through her veins. Visions flashed before her eyes, glimpses of her people, her family, and the hope that resided within their hearts. She knew that she had found a key, a vital piece of the puzzle that would lead her closer to salvation.

But the forest had one final trial in store—a guardian of shadows, a fearsome creature born of darkness itself. With piercing red eyes and a body that seemed to melt into the forest's depths, it blocked Jewel's path, snarling and hissing in defiance.

Summoning her courage, Jewel called upon the fragment of eternal love within her, its warmth surging through her being. She spoke words of compassion and understanding, reaching out to the guardian with a heart unclouded by fear. In that moment, the creature's eyes softened, its hostility giving way to recognition.

The guardian stepped aside, clearing the way for Jewel to continue her journey. As she ventured deeper into the heart of the Silver Forest, the guardian's eyes followed her, filled with a glimmer of hope and gratitude.

With each step forward, Jewel felt the weight of her mission and the love that fueled her purpose. The Heartstone nestled safely in her hands.

Chapter 4 Love's Resonance

Carrying the Heartstone, it's pulsating energy resonating with her every step, Jewel emerged from the depths of the Silver Forest. The guardian's eyes watched her departure, a newfound alliance forged between darkness and light. Now, with renewed determination, she embarked on the next phase of her quest.

Guided by the mystical map bestowed upon her by the Oracle, Jewel traversed vast landscapes, venturing through rugged mountains, vast plains, and winding rivers. The journey tested her endurance and resolve, but her heart remained steadfast in the pursuit of love's triumph over darkness.

As Jewel ventured deeper into the uncharted territories, whispers of her presence spread like tendrils in the wind. Rumors of her quest reached the ears of those who yearned for hope, and allies began to gather, drawn by the flickering light that emanated from her spirit.

Among the first to join her cause was Elara, a skilled archer with emerald eyes and a spirit as fiery as her arrows. Together, they faced formidable challenges, overcoming obstacles that sought to dampen their spirits. The bond they forged in battle was one of shared purpose, trust, and unyielding loyalty.

As Jewel and Elara continued their journey, they encountered villages ravaged by the encroaching darkness, their inhabitants desperate for salvation. The duo shared tales of eternal love, inspiring hope within hearts that had been plagued by despair. With each act of kindness and compassion, the light they carried grew brighter, gradually dispelling the shadows that threatened to engulf their world.

But not everyone welcomed their message of hope. A malevolent figure known as Malachi, a master of the dark arts, emerged from the depths of despair. He was drawn to Jewel's radiance, intent on extinguishing the flickering light that dared challenge his dominion.

Malachi, with his twisted smile and eyes that mirrored the abyss, unleashed his minions upon Jewel and Elara. Shadows writhed and twisted, seeking to snuff out their resolve. Yet, they stood strong, their spirits entwined with love's resilience.

Through battles fierce and fierce determination, Jewel and Elara prevailed, their unwavering bond an unbreakable shield against the forces of darkness. Their triumphs were not without sacrifice, as bruises marred their flesh and weariness settled in their bones. But they knew their journey was far from over, and they carried the scars as reminders of their resilience.

As they neared their destination, a sanctuary atop a mountaintop bathed in ethereal light, a beacon of hope amidst the encroaching darkness, Jewel and Elara felt the weight of their mission deep within their souls. The final confrontation with Malachi loomed, and their every step carried the burden of countless lives.

With the Heartstone clutched tightly in her grasp, Jewel ascended the steps of the sacred sanctuary, its pillars carved with symbols of love and unity. The air crackled with anticipation, energies intermingling, as Malachi emerged from the shadows, his malevolence palpable.

In a battle that would determine the fate of their world, Jewel and Elara fought with a fervor that could only be ignited by love's flame. The clash of opposing forces reverberated through the sacred halls, an echo of the cosmic struggle unfolding within their very beings.

With every strike, Jewel channeled the essence of eternal love, her heart resonating with the collective hopes and dreams of her people. Elara's arrows flew true, finding their mark with unwavering precision. Together, their unity forged an unbreakable shield against Malachi's dark sorcery.

Chapter 5 Triumph of Light

The brilliance of the Heartstone cascaded forth, engulfing the sacred sanctuary in a blinding, ethereal light. Its radiant glow pierced through the veil of darkness, illuminating every corner, banishing the shadows that clung to the walls.

Malachi, his malevolent power waning in the face of the Heartstone's radiance, recoiled, his eyes wide with disbelief and fury. The forces of darkness that had once obeyed his every command now trembled and faltered, unable to withstand the sheer power of love's triumph.

Jewel and Elara stood united, their hearts aligned with the eternal love that coursed through their veins. They advanced, their steps purposeful and resolute, driving Malachi further back into the depths of the sanctuary.

The sacred space vibrated with energy, as if acknowledging the climactic battle unfolding within its hallowed halls. The symbols etched upon the pillars seemed to pulse with life, lending strength to the champions of light.

With each strike and counterstrike, Jewel and Elara fought with unwavering determination, their movements an intricate dance of grace and power. Their weapons clashed against Malachi's dark sorcery, each blow reverberating with the resounding echoes of a world in desperate need of salvation.

As the battle raged on, Jewel could feel the weight of her people's hopes and dreams resting upon her shoulders. Their collective longing for peace and restoration fueled her resolve, lending her the strength to endure even the most relentless assaults from Malachi.

Elara's arrows flew with unparalleled precision, finding their mark in the heart of darkness. Her skill and unwavering aim proved to be an invaluable asset in the battle, her loyalty to Jewel serving as a steadfast pillar of support.

With one final surge of energy, Jewel unleashed a torrent of light, a culmination of her unwavering love and determination. It crashed against Malachi, shattering his dark fortress, and he stumbled backward, his power finally broken.

As the echoes of the battle subsided, silence settled over the sanctuary. Jewel and Elara stood tall, breathing heavily, their bodies bruised and weary but their spirits undeterred. The Heartstone still radiated with an iridescent glow, a testament to their triumph over darkness.

Approaching Malachi, Jewel extended a hand, her voice filled with a mixture of compassion and resolve. "It is not too late to turn away from darkness," she implored. "Embrace the light within you and find redemption."

Malachi's eyes flickered, his expression torn between defiance and a hint of remorse. For a moment, it seemed as if he might accept the offered hand, but then his features hardened, and he vanished into the depths of the sanctuary, consumed by his own pride and despair.

With a heavy sigh, Jewel turned to Elara, a mixture of relief and sorrow in her eyes. "Our battle is won, but the journey is far from over," she said, her voice tinged with determination. "We must now rally our allies, unite our people, and usher in a new era of light."

Elara nodded, a fire reigniting in her emerald eyes. "We will not falter," she affirmed. "Together, we shall build a future where love prevails over darkness, where hope is rekindled, and where our people can thrive once more."

With a shared understanding, Jewel and Elara left the sanctuary, their hearts filled with the knowledge that their triumph over Malachi was just the beginning. They would forge onward, gathering the scattered remnants of hope, and lead their people towards a brighter future, guided by the eternal flame of love that burned within their souls.

And so, their journey continued.

Chapter 6 A New Dawn

Jewel and Elara, united by their shared purpose and the triumph over Malachi, set forth on a mission to rally their allies and restore hope to their world. Word of their victory spread like wildfire, igniting the hearts of those who had been living in fear and uncertainty.

Villages and towns, once shrouded in darkness, began to stir with newfound determination. The people, inspired by the tale of love's triumph, gathered in eager anticipation, ready to lend their support to the cause. From every corner of the realm, they came together, each person carrying a flickering flame symbolizing their unwavering belief in a brighter future.

Jewel and Elara stood before the gathered multitude, their faces adorned with scars and their spirits fortified by the battles they had overcome. The Heartstone, still pulsating with radiant energy, rested at the center of a makeshift altar—a beacon of hope and a reminder of the power of love.

Addressing the crowd, Jewel's voice resonated with strength and conviction. "We stand here today, united by a common purpose—to reclaim our world from the clutches of darkness and restore the light that has been overshadowed for far too long. Together, we will forge a path towards a future where love prevails and peace reigns."

The crowd erupted into cheers, their voices mingling in a resounding chorus of hope. The time for action had arrived, and Jewel knew that the path ahead would be arduous, but she was bolstered by the unwavering support of her people.

Under Jewel and Elara's guidance, a network of resistance formed—a tapestry woven with threads of courage, resilience, and love. They strategized, utilizing the unique strengths of each individual to counter the lingering remnants of darkness that still threatened their world.

The united force embarked on missions to reclaim territories once dominated by Malachi's influence. With unwavering determination, they faced trials and tribulations, battling both physical adversaries and the inner demons that threatened to dim their resolve. But with every victory, the flame of hope burned brighter, illuminating the path forward.

As their journey progressed, Jewel discovered the true extent of her abilities. She possessed a gift for channeling the energy of the Heartstone, weaving its power into protective barriers and healing energies. With each act of love and compassion, her connection to the eternal flame grew stronger, guiding her steps and illuminating her path.

Elara, too, discovered her own hidden depths. Her unparalleled archery skills were honed further, her arrows guided by an intuitive understanding of the battle between light and darkness. She became a beacon of inspiration for those who sought to harness their individual strengths in service of the greater good.

Together, Jewel and Elara forged an unbreakable bond, their spirits entwined in a dance of trust and camaraderie. Their partnership symbolized the unification of love and resilience, an embodiment of the undying spirit that refused to yield in the face of adversity.

As they continued to dismantle the remnants of darkness, piece by piece, hope blossomed in the hearts of their people. The realm, once gripped by despair, embraced the promise of a new dawn—an era where the echoes of eternal love reverberated through every corner, infusing the land with warmth and healing.

With time, the realm flourished once more. Vibrant colors painted the landscapes, laughter echoed through the streets, and a sense of harmony prevailed. The wounds inflicted by darkness began to heal, and the scars became a testament to the resilience of the human spirit.

Jewel and Elara's quest had transformed not only their own lives but also the destiny of their world. Their story became legend—a tale whispered among generations.

Chapter 7 The Legacy of Eternal Love

Years had passed since the defeat of Malachi and the restoration of light to the realm. Jewel and Elara, now revered as heroes, continued their tireless efforts to nurture and safeguard the legacy of eternal love.

The realm thrived under their guidance, with peace and prosperity becoming the norm. The people, united by a shared vision, built a society that valued compassion, empathy, and the pursuit of knowledge. Schools flourished, where children learned not only the arts and sciences but also the values of love and kindness.

Jewel and Elara established the Eternal Love Academy, a place dedicated to the study and cultivation of love's transformative power. The academy welcomed individuals from all walks of life, fostering an environment where they could explore their own inner light and learn to harness the energy of love for the greater good.

Students at the academy delved into the teachings of ancient wisdom, honing their abilities to channel love's energy. They studied healing arts, mastering techniques that brought solace to the wounded and the broken-hearted. They also developed ways to extend love's reach beyond their realm, offering aid to neighboring lands in need.

Jewel and Elara's influence extended beyond the academy. They traveled far and wide, sharing their wisdom, and spreading the message of love's transformative power. Their words resonated with leaders and communities alike, igniting a global movement that sought to eradicate darkness and replace it with the warmth of love.

But their work was not without challenges. Although the forces of darkness had been vanquished, remnants lingered in the hearts of some who had once been swayed by Malachi's seductive promises. Jewel and Elara recognized that true change could only come from within and embarked on a mission to heal those who still clung to the vestiges of darkness.

They journeyed to distant lands, meeting individuals whose hearts were burdened by anger, fear, and pain. With patience and unwavering love, they offered guidance, helping these lost souls find solace and rediscover the light that resided within. One by one, hearts were mended, and seeds of love took root.

As the years passed, Jewel and Elara's mortal lives drew to a close. Their physical forms aged gracefully, their hair streaked with silver, and their faces etched with lines that spoke of a life well-lived. But their spirits remained vibrant and their love undiminished.

On the eve of their passing, Jewel and Elara called upon their most trusted disciples and shared their final wisdom. They imparted the importance of unity, reminding their followers that love transcended time and boundaries, and that the responsibility to carry forth the flame of eternal love rested with each individual.

With heavy hearts, their disciples bid them farewell, vowing to honor their teachings and protect the legacy they had built. Jewel and Elara departed from the mortal realm, their spirits merging with the eternal flame of love, forever guiding and inspiring those who walked in their footsteps.

The realm mourned their loss but celebrated their lives and the legacy they had left behind. The Eternal Love Academy continued to flourish, producing generations of compassionate leaders, healers, and champions of love. The realm prospered under their care, an enduring testament to the transformative power of love.

And so, the story of Jewel and Elara became legend—a tale of two souls who had journeyed through darkness to reclaim the light. Their names were etched in the annals of history, a reminder that love, when nurtured and shared, had the power to shape destinies and weave a tapestry of unity across the realms.

And as the sun set on each day, casting a golden glow upon the land, the people would look to the sky, their hearts filled with joy and love for their world.

Chapter 8 An Everlasting Flame

Generations passed, and the realm continued to thrive, illuminated by the everlasting flame of eternal love. The teachings of Jewel and Elara echoed through the ages, carried on the lips of storytellers and etched within the hearts of the people. Their tale became a guiding light, a reminder of the power that resided within each individual to shape their own destiny.

The Eternal Love Academy stood as a beacon of wisdom and enlightenment, nurturing souls who sought to deepen their understanding of love's transformative energy. The academy's halls echoed with laughter, passionate discussions, and the exchange of knowledge as students from all walks of life came together in pursuit of a greater purpose.

The disciples who had once learned directly from Jewel and Elara became revered mentors themselves, passing down the teachings of love to the next generation. They carried the flame forward, fanning its warmth and radiance to all corners of the realm.

Beyond the borders of their realm, the legacy of eternal love had spread, influencing neighboring lands and fostering connections that transcended boundaries. The realm had become a beacon of hope and inspiration, drawing seekers of love and enlightenment from far and wide.

In this era of peace, a young girl named Aurora emerged, her heart burning with a desire to carry on the mission of eternal love. She possessed a rare gift—the ability to hear the whispers of the Heartstone itself, guiding her with its gentle voice and illuminating her path.

Aurora, guided by her deep connection to the eternal flame, followed in the footsteps of Jewel and Elara. She embraced her role as a protector of love, standing as a guardian of compassion and unity in a world that still faced its own trials.

With the knowledge imparted by the Eternal Love Academy and the wisdom of her predecessors, Aurora embarked on her own journey, reaching out to those in need and weaving love's transformative power into every corner she touched.

She traveled to lands far and wide, encountering individuals who had lost their way, their hearts burdened by doubt and fear. With empathy and understanding, Aurora extended a hand, helping them rediscover the love that had always resided within. Her mere presence infused hope and ignited a spark within each soul she encountered.

Aurora's reputation grew, and her influence spread like wildfire, inspiring countless others to rise and embrace the call of eternal love. Together, they formed a network of love warriors, united in their mission to heal and transform the world through acts of kindness, compassion, and understanding.

The realm, now spanning across continents and cultures, embraced the teachings of love as the foundation of their society. Laws were shaped with empathy, and governance was guided by a collective sense of responsibility and care for all beings.

As Aurora journeyed through life, she carried the wisdom and love of her predecessors within her, continuing the cycle of love's transmission. She knew that the flame of eternal love could never be extinguished as long as there were hearts willing to embrace its warmth.

And so, the tale of eternal love continued to unfold, an ever-evolving symphony of compassion and unity. The realm and its people danced to the rhythm of love's song, each individual adding their unique notes to the harmonious melody.

In the hearts of all who carried the flame, the spirit of Jewel and Elara lived on—a reminder that love had the power to transcend time and create a legacy that would endure for eternity.

And as the sun set on each day, casting a golden glow upon the land, the people looked to the sky, their hearts filled with gratitude and reverence for the everlasting flame that had guided their path. They knew that as long as love burned within them, their world would forever be bathed in the radiance of eternal love.

Chapter 9 The Celestial Union

In the realm touched by the eternal flame of love, a new era dawned, marked by an extraordinary event—a celestial union that would bridge the realms and bring together the forces of light from across the cosmos.

As the cycles of time turned, aligning the stars in a rare celestial dance, whispers spread through the realm. It was said that on this auspicious night, the convergence of cosmic energies would open a gateway, allowing beings from distant realms to unite in a celebration of love and unity.

Preparations were made with great anticipation, as the realm's inhabitants eagerly awaited the arrival of visitors from other realms. The Eternal Love Academy became a hub of activity, hosting emissaries and scholars who sought to share their wisdom and learn from the realm's profound connection to love.

Aurora, now a wise and revered guardian, stood at the forefront of the preparations. She worked tirelessly, coordinating the arrangements and ensuring that every aspect of the event would embody the essence of eternal love.

As the day of the celestial union approached, the realm shimmered with an otherworldly energy. The skies glowed with hues of cerulean, magenta, and gold, as if the heavens themselves were preparing to witness the harmonious convergence of worlds.

The visitors arrived, their presence heralded by a radiant light that touched every corner of the realm. They were beings of immense beauty and grace, representing a myriad of realms and dimensions. Each carried within them the wisdom and love of their own worlds, eager to share and learn from the realm blessed by the eternal flame.

A grand ceremony unfolded, with music, dance, and vibrant displays of artistry. Beings from all realms intertwined their energies, creating a symphony of love that resonated throughout the cosmos. The barriers that separated their worlds dissolved, as they basked in the shared understanding of love's transformative power.

In the heart of the ceremony, Aurora stood before the gathered multitude, her voice carrying a melody that spoke to the depths of their souls. She spoke of the realm's journey, of the trials faced and the triumphs achieved through the power of love. Her words touched the hearts of all, weaving a tapestry of unity and connection among the realms.

As the celestial union reached its climax, a burst of radiant energy emanated from the center, encompassing all beings present. It was a fusion of light, love, and wisdom—a divine alchemy that merged the collective consciousness of the realms into a harmonious whole.

In this moment of transcendent unity, the barriers between realms dissolved entirely. Beings from different worlds, once separated by vast distances, embraced one another, their energies blending in a symphony of love that echoed through the cosmos.

From this union, a profound realization emerged—the understanding that love was the common thread that wove through all existence. It was the eternal flame that burned within every being, and it had the power to heal, transform, and bring forth a future where all realms were united in peace and harmony.

With hearts aglow, the beings bid farewell to one another, carrying with them the memories and lessons of the celestial union. They returned to their realms, forever changed, and spread the message of love, radiating its warmth and illuminating the path for others to follow.

In the realm touched by the eternal flame, a deep sense of fulfillment settled within the hearts of its inhabitants. They knew that their connection to the greater cosmos was solidified, and that the legacy of eternal love would continue to evolve and inspire future generations.

Aurora, now a luminous symbol of hope and unity, continued her mission as a guardian of love. She guided the realm forward, nurturing the flames of love that burned brightly within each individual.

Chapter 10 The Eternal Flame Rekindled

In the wake of the celestial union, the realm flourished, basking in the transformative power of love. The teachings of the eternal flame resonated deeply within the hearts of its inhabitants, guiding their actions and shaping the very fabric of their society.

Aurora, now revered as the Keeper of the Eternal Flame, stood as a beacon of love and wisdom. Her presence radiated warmth and compassion, drawing people from far and wide seeking guidance and solace. She embraced her role with humility, knowing that the flame she carried belonged to all.

Under Aurora's guidance, the Eternal Love Academy expanded its reach, welcoming individuals from realms near and far who sought to deepen their understanding of love's essence. The academy became a haven of learning, where knowledge was shared, and souls were nurtured.

Students from various realms gathered at the academy, their hearts ablaze with a shared purpose—to embody love in its purest form and spread its transformative energy across the cosmos. They delved into ancient texts, explored the arts, and honed their abilities to heal and inspire through acts of love and kindness.

As the years passed, the teachings of the Eternal Flame found their way into every corner of the realm. Communities embraced love as their guiding principle, fostering unity, compassion, and understanding. Love flowed through the veins of the realm, connecting its inhabitants in a profound web of interconnectedness.

Beyond the realm, the influence of eternal love continued to expand. Beings from other realms, touched by the stories of the celestial union, embarked on their own journeys of discovery and transformation. They carried the flame of love within them, igniting sparks of compassion wherever they traveled.

In the realm's darkest moments, when the shadows threatened to encroach upon the light, the inhabitants stood steadfast, drawing upon the collective strength of their love. They understood that the journey of eternal love was not without its challenges, but they faced them with unwavering faith and resilience.

Aurora, wise and serene, remained the embodiment of love's guiding light. She continued to inspire, guiding the realm's leaders, healers, and visionaries, reminding them of the transformative power that resided within their hearts.

One fateful day, as Aurora stood at the precipice of the realm, gazing out into the vast cosmos, she felt a surge of energy ripple through her being. It was as if the very essence of the eternal flame stirred within her, urging her to embark on a new journey.

With a gentle smile, Aurora turned to her beloved companions—the disciples who had journeyed with her throughout the ages—and shared her revelation. Together, they understood that it was time to carry the flame of eternal love beyond the boundaries of their realm and into the uncharted territories of the cosmos.

Leaving behind a legacy of love and unity, the disciples bid farewell to their beloved realm, their hearts filled with gratitude for the lessons learned and the connections forged. They embarked on a cosmic voyage, guided by the eternal flame that burned brightly within each of them.

Their mission was clear—to kindle the spark of love in realms that had long been overshadowed by darkness, to heal wounded hearts, and to reunite scattered souls under the banner of eternal love.

As they traversed the cosmos, encountering realms teetering on the brink of despair, the disciples became beacons of hope. They shared stories of the realm they had left behind, tales of unity, compassion, and the unwavering power of love.

With each realm they touched, the flame of eternal love grew stronger, illuminating the darkest corners and inspiring beings to rise above their struggles. The disciples witnessed the transformation that unfolded, as love's gentle touch melted away the barriers that had kept communities divided and hearts disconnected.

Chapter 11 The Return of the Beloved

In the depths of the cosmos, where stars danced and nebulae swirled, the disciples of eternal love continued their cosmic voyage, carrying the flame of love to realms yearning for its healing touch. Their journey had been long and filled with both triumphs and challenges, but their resolve remained unwavering.

As they traveled, word spread of their mission, and realms eagerly awaited their arrival, eager to bask in the radiance of eternal love. The disciples arrived in each realm with open hearts, extending a hand of friendship and understanding, and sharing the timeless teachings that had guided their own realm.

In every realm they encountered, the transformative power of love worked its magic. Barriers crumbled, as hearts once burdened by darkness embraced the light of compassion. Communities united, setting aside their differences and focusing on the shared bond of love that connected them all.

One such realm, a world plagued by years of conflict and strife, stood on the precipice of despair. The disciples arrived with hearts brimming with hope, determined to ignite the flame of love within every soul they encountered. They listened to the stories of pain and loss, offering comfort and understanding.

Through their presence and guidance, the disciples helped the realm's inhabitants recognize their shared humanity and the power of love to heal wounds that had festered for far too long. Slowly but surely, a transformation took place—a renaissance of love and unity that spread like wildfire.

In the midst of this healing, a figure emerged—a beloved soul who had long been lost in the darkness. His name was Aiden, a gifted poet and philosopher whose heart had been consumed by bitterness and anger. Aiden had watched from the shadows as his realm suffered, unable to find solace or hope.

But with the arrival of the disciples and their unwavering commitment to love, something stirred within Aiden's weary soul. He felt a glimmer of light penetrate the depths of his being, rekindling a long-forgotten ember of hope. Drawn to their teachings, he approached the disciples, his heart heavy with the weight of his past.

The disciples, recognizing Aiden's thirst for redemption and transformation, welcomed him with open arms. They listened to his words, witnessing the pain and sorrow etched upon his face. With love and compassion, they offered him guidance, showing him that even the darkest corners of his heart could be illuminated by love's gentle touch.

In the days that followed, Aiden immersed himself in the teachings of eternal love, absorbing every word with an insatiable hunger for change. Through reflection and introspection, he began to peel away the layers of bitterness and resentment that had enveloped him.

As he embraced the power of forgiveness and self-love, Aiden's words blossomed into verses of beauty and grace.

His poetry spoke of the human experience—the joy, the pain, the longing—and the transformative power of love to heal even the deepest wounds.

The realm, witnessing Aiden's transformation, was captivated by his words and drawn to his newfound light. His poetry became a beacon of hope, inspiring others to embark on their own journeys of self-discovery and love.

In time, Aiden's influence grew, and he emerged as a voice of wisdom and compassion, guiding the realm towards a future grounded in love and understanding. His words became a soothing balm for those who had known only suffering, and his presence ignited a spark of hope in hearts that had long been overshadowed by despair.

As the disciples prepared to leave the realm, their mission fulfilled, Aiden stood before them, gratitude shining in his eyes. He expressed his deepest gratitude for their unwavering love and support, recognizing that without their guidance, he may have remained lost in the shadows forever.

With heartfelt farewells, the disciples departed, their cosmic voyage continuing. They carried with them the memory of Aiden's transformation, a testament to the power of love to heal even the most wounded souls.

In the realm they left behind, Aiden continued to spread the teachings of eternal love, his words resonating with all who heard them. The realm, once consumed by darkness, now glowed with the warmth of love's embrace, forever changed by the return of their beloved poet.

And so, the journey of eternal love continued, as the disciples traversed the cosmos, their hearts aflame with the knowledge that love's transformative power knew no bounds. With each realm they touched, they left behind a legacy of unity, compassion, and the unwavering belief that love could heal and unite even the most fractured of worlds.

Chapter 12 The Everlasting Legacy

In the wake of their cosmic voyage, the disciples of eternal love found themselves at a pivotal moment—the culmination of their journey and the beginning of a new chapter in the realm of love. They returned to their cherished realm, their hearts brimming with stories of transformation and unity.

As they stepped foot on familiar ground, they were greeted with joyous celebrations and a profound sense of gratitude. The realm had flourished in their absence, guided by the wisdom and teachings they had shared before their departure.

Aurora, the steadfast guardian of the Eternal Flame, stood at the center of the festivities. Her radiant presence filled the air, reminding all of the eternal nature of love and the limitless potential it held. She commended the disciples for their unwavering dedication and the profound impact they had made on realms far and wide.

In the following days, the disciples shared their experiences and the lessons they had learned during their cosmic voyage. Their stories of love's transformative power touched the hearts of all who listened, inspiring a renewed commitment to embody the principles of eternal love.

In the realm's newly expanded Eternal Love Academy, disciples and inhabitants alike gathered to learn from one another. The realm had become a vibrant hub of knowledge and understanding, where the pursuit of love's wisdom was revered above all else.

Under the guidance of Aurora and the disciples, the academy became a sanctuary for souls seeking to deepen their connection to love. Students immersed themselves in the teachings, exploring various paths to express and embody love in their lives.

Within the academy's walls, disciplines such as healing, art, music, and philosophy flourished. Scholars and practitioners from far and wide were drawn to the realm, eager to share their wisdom and learn from the realm's profound connection to eternal love.

The disciples, now revered as mentors and leaders, guided and nurtured the academy's students. They shared the stories of their cosmic voyage, imparting the invaluable lessons they had learned from realms beyond their own. The students listened with rapt attention, their hearts open to the wisdom that flowed through the words of their beloved mentors.

As the years passed, the realm became a beacon of love and unity, known throughout the cosmos for its unwavering commitment to the eternal flame. Beings from distant realms sought solace and guidance within its borders, knowing that here they would find a sanctuary where love's transformative power was honored and celebrated.

The teachings of eternal love spread like wildfire, carried on the wings of the realm's inhabitants who ventured beyond its borders. Love became a language spoken across realms, bridging divides and nurturing connections. The disciples' legacy grew, extending far beyond the realm they called home.

In the annals of cosmic history, the realm's journey stood as a testament to the boundless potential of love. Its inhabitants, guided by the eternal flame, had transcended their limitations and awakened to the profound truth that love was the very fabric of existence.

And so, the realm of eternal love thrived, forever radiating its light and warmth across the cosmos. Its inhabitants, united by the eternal flame, continued to write the story of love's transformative power, ensuring that its legacy would endure for all eternity.

In the realm's heart, Aurora stood, her gaze filled with love and hope. She knew that the disciples had fulfilled their sacred mission, igniting a flame of love that would forever burn bright in the hearts of all who embraced its call. With gratitude and a renewed sense of purpose, she whispered a silent vow—to nurture the realm's eternal love, ensuring that its legacy would endure for generations to come.

And in that moment, the realm stood as a testament to the eternal nature of love, a beacon of hope, and a reminder to all that within the depths of every heart, the flame of love would forever flicker, illuminating the path to unity, healing, and everlasting joy.

Chapter 13 The Cosmic Reunion

Deep within the fabric of the cosmos, where stars twinkled and galaxies spun, a cosmic reunion was set to unfold. The disciples of eternal love, having spread the flame of love to countless realms, felt an undeniable pull to gather once more in the realm they had called home.

As if guided by an unseen force, the disciples embarked on a journey back to the realm of eternal love. Excitement filled their hearts as they anticipated the joyous reunion and the opportunity to share the stories of their cosmic voyage with one another.

Word of their imminent return spread like wildfire throughout the realm, and anticipation grew among its inhabitants. The realm hummed with an electric energy, as hearts brimmed with love, unity, and the longing to reconnect with those who had ventured into the farthest reaches of the cosmos.

The day of the reunion arrived, and the realm's vibrant landscapes shimmered with a renewed radiance. Its inhabitants, dressed in colorful attire, gathered at the heart of the realm, where a grand amphitheater had been prepared for the occasion.

Aurora, the revered guardian of the eternal flame, stood at the center of the amphitheater, her presence emanating a serene grace. Her eyes sparkled with joy as she welcomed the disciples, who approached one by one, their faces alight with anticipation and love.

With each disciple's arrival, a chorus of cheers and applause filled the air, echoing through the realm. Hugs were exchanged, tears of joy were shed, and heartfelt words of gratitude filled the space. The reunion was a celebration of the profound bond they shared—a bond forged through the transformative power of love.

As the disciples settled into their places, Aurora stood before them, her voice carrying a sense of wisdom and reverence. She spoke of their cosmic voyage, weaving together the stories and experiences they had accumulated, illustrating the vast impact they had made on countless realms.

Tales of realms once shrouded in darkness but now illuminated by the flame of eternal love were shared. Stories of hearts healed, communities united, and the resilience of love in the face of adversity resonated deeply with all who listened.

In the midst of the storytelling, a hush fell upon the amphitheater as a figure emerged from the crowd—a being of radiant light and familiar presence. It was Aiden, the beloved poet who had undergone his own transformative journey. With a twinkle in his eyes and a smile upon his lips, he stepped forward to share his own tale.

Aiden's voice filled the amphitheater, his words flowing like a melody, carrying the essence of love's transformative power. He spoke of his path from bitterness to forgiveness, from darkness to light. His poetry wove a tapestry of emotions, touching the deepest recesses of every heart present.

The realm's inhabitants listened in awe, their souls stirred by the beauty and wisdom that flowed through Aiden's words. They recognized themselves in his story, seeing their own journeys reflected in the tapestry he painted with his poetry.

As Aiden concluded his tale, a thunderous applause erupted, reverberating through the realm. It was a recognition of his courage, his resilience, and his unwavering commitment to the path of eternal love.

The reunion continued with moments of shared laughter, heartfelt conversations, and the exchange of knowledge and wisdom. The disciples embraced their fellow inhabitants, rejoicing in the bonds forged through their shared experiences and love for one another.

As the sun dipped below the horizon, painting the sky with hues of gold and crimson, the reunion reached its culmination. Aurora, standing once more at the center of the amphitheater, raised her hands, calling for silence.

With a voice filled with love and gratitude, she expressed her deepest appreciation to the disciples for their unwavering dedication, their courage, and their unyielding commitment to the path of eternal love. She recognized that their journey had not been without challenges, but their resilience and faith had carried them through.

As the disciples stood before her, their hearts overflowing with love, Aurora bestowed upon them a sacred honor— the Eternal Flame Medallion. Crafted from the purest essence of love, the medallion symbolized their eternal connection to the flame and their role as ambassadors of love in the cosmos.

With tears of joy and renewed purpose, the disciples accepted the medallions, feeling a surge of love's power course through their beings. They knew that their journey, though forever evolving, would continue, for the flame of eternal love would forever burn brightly within their hearts.

And so, the cosmic reunion drew to a close, leaving behind a trail of love, unity, and inspiration in its wake. The disciples returned to the realms they had visited, carrying with them the joyous memories of the reunion and the unwavering belief that love would forever guide their paths.

In the realm of eternal love, its inhabitants basked in the warmth and radiance of the eternal flame, their hearts forever transformed by the cosmic reunion. They knew that love's legacy would endure, weaving its way through the fabric of the cosmos, bringing healing, unity, and eternal joy to all who embraced its divine embrace.

Chapter 14 The Tapestry of Love

In the realm of eternal love, a profound stillness settled in the wake of the cosmic reunion. The disciples, having returned from their journeys, felt a sense of fulfillment and gratitude for the transformative experiences they had encountered.

With hearts brimming with love and wisdom, the disciples gathered in the sacred Grove of Reflection—a tranquil oasis within the realm. Surrounded by ancient trees and fragrant blossoms, they sat in a circle, each one sharing the lessons and insights they had gained during their cosmic voyage.

As they took turns speaking, the air became charged with a sense of reverence. Each disciple's voice wove a unique thread into the tapestry of love, painting a vivid picture of the transformative power they had witnessed.

Luna, whose gentle presence had comforted many realms, spoke of the importance of self-love as the foundation for all other forms of love. She shared stories of beings who had discovered their worth and embraced their authentic selves, finding liberation in the acceptance of their true essence.

Sol, the embodiment of radiant strength, shared tales of communities uniting in the face of adversity. He spoke of the power of love to bridge divides, dissolve prejudice, and build bridges of understanding. Through his stories, he emphasized that even the smallest acts of kindness could create ripples of change in the vast cosmic ocean.

Aria, the compassionate healer, spoke of the profound impact of love's touch on wounded hearts and broken spirits. She recounted tales of souls who had found solace in love's embrace, their pain transformed into resilience and their wounds transformed into wisdom. Her words were a reminder that love had the power to heal even the deepest scars.

Elias, the visionary artist, shared his experiences of love's ability to transcend boundaries and touch the depths of the soul. He spoke of the beauty that emerged from the fusion of diverse perspectives, emphasizing the importance of celebrating individuality while recognizing the interconnectedness of all beings.

As the disciples continued to share their stories, the tapestry of love grew richer and more intricate. Each thread woven into the fabric represented a realm touched by their presence, a soul awakened to the eternal flame burning within.

In the midst of their sharing, Aurora, the guardian of the eternal flame, appeared before them. Her presence exuded a timeless grace, and her eyes shone with an otherworldly light.

"Beloved disciples," Aurora began, her voice resonating with a wisdom that transcended time and space, "your journeys have been remarkable, and your commitment to the path of eternal love unwavering. But remember, love's work is never truly complete. It is a journey that continues to unfold, revealing new depths and mysteries with each step."

She paused, her gaze sweeping across the circle, meeting the eyes of each disciple. "Now, as you sit here, sharing the stories of your journeys, I invite you to reflect upon the tapestry of love you have woven together. Each thread represents a life touched, a heart awakened, and a world forever changed."

With a wave of her hand, the Grove of Reflection transformed, the trees shimmering with a kaleidoscope of colors. Within the branches, the tapestry of love manifested, its vibrant threads shimmering in the gentle breeze.

The disciples gazed in awe at the tapestry, feeling a profound connection to its intricate patterns. They saw the souls they had encountered, the challenges they had faced, and the love that had blossomed in even the darkest corners.

Aurora continued, "As you behold this tapestry, remember that your journey is not confined to the realms you have visited. Love's call is eternal, and its reach is boundless. Let the tapestry serve as a reminder of the interconnectedness of all beings and the infinite possibilities that lie within the embrace of eternal love."

With a final smile, Aurora vanished, leaving the disciples to contemplate the tapestry before them. In its vibrant colors and intricate patterns, they saw their purpose and their destiny—to continue weaving the threads of love, to touch lives, and to be the conduits of love's transformative power.

And so, the disciples sat in the Grove of Reflection, their hearts united in a shared vision. They knew that their journey had only just begun, and that together, they would continue to illuminate the cosmos with the radiant flame of eternal love.

Chapter 15 The Celestial Symphony

In the realm of eternal love, a harmonious stillness permeated the air. The disciples, having reflected upon the tapestry of love, felt a renewed sense of purpose and unity. They knew that their individual journeys had merged into a collective mission—to create a symphony of love that would resonate throughout the cosmos.

Guided by their shared vision, the disciples gathered in the Heart of Unity, a sacred chamber pulsating with the essence of love. The chamber was adorned with shimmering crystals and exquisite tapestries, representing the diversity and interconnectedness of all beings.

As they entered, a gentle melody floated through the chamber, its ethereal notes weaving a spell of serenity and anticipation. The disciples took their places in a circular formation, their eyes reflecting the flickering flames of the Eternal Flame at the center.

Silence descended upon the chamber, as if the entire realm held its breath in anticipation. Then, from the depths of their souls, the disciples began to sing. Each voice carried a unique timbre, yet their melodies intertwined seamlessly, creating a celestial harmony that reverberated throughout the chamber.

The chamber filled with a cascade of sound, a symphony of love that transcended language and touched the core of every being present. It was a symphony that embraced the beauty of diversity and celebrated the unity that existed within all hearts.

As their voices soared, the disciples felt a profound connection, as if they were not merely singing together, but merging their essence to become a singular force of love. They could sense the ripple of their harmonious vibrations spreading beyond the realm, permeating the cosmic tapestry of existence.

In the midst of their symphony, the chamber pulsed with an otherworldly light. Aurora, the guardian of the eternal flame, appeared at the center of the circle. Her presence amplified the resonance of their voices, infusing them with a radiant energy.

With a voice that seemed to encompass the cosmos, Aurora spoke, "Beloved disciples, your harmonious symphony reverberates through the realms, transcending time and space. Your unity is a testament to the power of love, a reminder that when hearts join in harmony, miracles unfold."

She extended her hand, and as if in response, the chamber transformed. The walls dissolved, revealing a panoramic view of the cosmos. Stars glittered like diamonds, galaxies spun in graceful dances, and celestial beings gathered to witness the celestial symphony of love.

Aurora continued, her voice a melodic embrace, "Let your symphony of love be a beacon of hope, guiding lost souls back to the path of love. Let it inspire realms far and wide to embrace unity, compassion, and the transformative power of love."

The disciples sang with renewed fervor, their voices reaching celestial heights. With every note, love's vibration grew stronger, resonating with the hearts of all who listened. The celestial beings joined in, their ethereal voices blending seamlessly with those of the disciples.

As the symphony reached its crescendo, a surge of pure love emanated from the Heart of Unity, cascading through the cosmos. Realms once shrouded in darkness were bathed in a radiant light, and hearts once burdened by strife were filled with renewed hope and joy.

As the final note echoed through the chamber, a profound stillness settled upon the realm. The disciples, their voices now hushed, gazed at one another, their eyes reflecting the depth of their shared experience.

Aurora smiled, her eyes sparkling with pride. "Beloved disciples," she whispered, "you have woven a symphony of love that shall echo throughout eternity. Embrace this unity, cherish this connection, and continue to be the conduits of love's transformative power."

And so, in the realm of eternal love, the disciples stood united, their voices forever entwined in the celestial symphony. They knew that their journey would continue, for the symphony of love had only just begun, and its harmonious melody would guide them towards new horizons of love, compassion, and unity.

Chapter 16 The Infinite Tapestry

In the realm of eternal love, a sense of fulfillment and purpose settled upon the disciples. Their voices had woven a symphony of love that resonated through the cosmos, touching hearts and transforming lives. Now, as they gathered once more, a new calling beckoned them—a quest to discover the infinite tapestry of love.

Guided by their shared vision, the disciples embarked on a journey beyond the boundaries of their realm. They traversed vast cosmic landscapes, venturing into uncharted realms and encountering beings of extraordinary wisdom and love.

With each step, their hearts expanded, their understanding deepened, and their connection to the eternal flame grew stronger. They witnessed love manifesting in countless forms—a gentle touch, a selfless act, a smile that warmed the soul. They understood that love was not confined to a single realm but flowed through the very fabric of the universe.

As they traveled, the disciples encountered realms where love had been forgotten, overshadowed by fear, pain, and division. With unwavering determination, they infused these realms with the radiant flame of eternal love, mending fractured hearts and restoring the bonds of unity.

In the realm of shadows, they met a lost soul named Amara—a being once consumed by darkness but yearning for the embrace of love. Through their compassion and unwavering support, they guided Amara towards the path of healing, teaching her that love had the power to illuminate even the darkest corners of the soul.

In the realm of dreams, they encountered a realm where love flourished in ethereal forms—a dance of moonlight, a whisper of wind, a gentle caress of starlight. Here, they celebrated the beauty of love's infinite expressions, inspiring the inhabitants to cherish the magic that love bestowed upon their lives.

In the realm of unity, they witnessed diverse beings coexisting in harmony, their hearts intertwined by a deep understanding of their shared humanity. Here, the disciples learned that love had the power to dissolve boundaries and bridge differences, reminding them of the universal connection that bound all beings.

With each realm they encountered, the disciples added a new thread to the infinite tapestry of love. The tapestry grew more vibrant, its patterns expanding with every act of kindness, every moment of compassion, and every choice made in the name of love.

As they journeyed, the disciples also discovered that the tapestry was not static but ever-evolving. It embraced the experiences of all beings, weaving their stories into its intricate design. It reminded them that love's work was not confined to a single realm or a single moment, but an ongoing commitment to nurturing and expanding the flame of eternal love.

In their encounters, the disciples saw reflections of themselves—their struggles, their triumphs, their vulnerabilities, and their strengths. They recognized that the journey of love was a collective one, and that by uplifting others, they too were uplifted.

And so, with hearts ablaze, the disciples returned to the realm of eternal love, carrying with them the wisdom and love they had gathered from their cosmic voyage. They stood before the eternal flame, their souls resonating with the infinite tapestry they had contributed to.

Aurora, the guardian of the eternal flame, appeared before them, her presence a radiant glow. Her voice carried the weight of infinite love as she spoke, "Beloved disciples, you have embarked on a journey that has expanded your understanding and deepened your connection to the tapestry of love. Embrace the truth that love knows no bounds, that its power extends far beyond the realms you have visited."

She continued, her words echoing in their hearts, "Remember, the tapestry of love is ever-growing, ever-evolving. It is a testament to the beauty and resilience of the human spirit, a reminder that love's essence can be found in every moment, every interaction, and every choice made with an open heart."

As Aurora faded into the radiant flames, the disciples stood in awe, their souls alight with purpose. They knew that their journey would continue, their quest to explore the infinite tapestry of love far from over. With renewed determination, they vowed to continue weaving the threads of love, for the tapestry of love was an eternal masterpiece, forever expanding, forever embracing the souls that dared to journey in its name.

Chapter 17 The Essence Within

In the realm of eternal love, the disciples found themselves immersed in a profound stillness. The cosmic voyage had revealed to them the vastness of love's tapestry, but now they sought to explore a deeper truth—the essence of love that resided within each and every being.

Guided by their innate curiosity and a yearning for greater understanding, the disciples embarked on an inward journey, delving into the depths of their own hearts. They sought to uncover the essence of love that dwelled within them and to nurture its radiance, knowing that by doing so, they would illuminate the path for others.

They retreated to a sacred sanctuary, a tranquil space nestled within the realm, where they could engage in introspection and commune with the eternal flame. Surrounded by the gentle flickering light, they closed their eyes, allowing their breath to deepen and their minds to quiet.

In the stillness of their meditation, the disciples discovered a radiant presence—a profound sense of love that emanated from within. It was not a love born of external circumstances or attachments, but a love that simply was—an intrinsic part of their being.

With each breath, the disciples embraced this love, allowing it to flow through them and permeate every aspect of their existence. They recognized that by connecting with the essence of love within themselves, they could awaken the same essence in others, igniting a chain reaction of love's transformative power.

As they delved deeper, the disciples encountered the shadows that lingered within their hearts—the doubts, fears, and insecurities that threatened to obscure their inner light. With compassion and courage, they faced these shadows, offering them love and acceptance, recognizing that love's essence could embrace both light and darkness.

In this sacred sanctuary, the disciples engaged in practices that nurtured their connection to the essence of love. They engaged in acts of self-care and self-compassion, recognizing that by loving themselves unconditionally, they could radiate that love outward to the world.

They practiced forgiveness, releasing the weight of past grievances and allowing love to heal old wounds. They cultivated gratitude, recognizing the blessings and beauty that surrounded them, and extended love's embrace to all beings.

In their daily interactions, the disciples became living embodiments of love's essence. They listened deeply to others, offering their presence and understanding. They offered acts of kindness and generosity, knowing that even the smallest gestures could have a profound impact.

Through their continued journey of self-discovery, the disciples began to witness the transformation that love's essence sparked within themselves and those they encountered. Hearts once burdened by sorrow and strife found solace in the warmth of their presence. Souls once lost and disconnected rediscovered their inherent worth and interconnectedness.

As the disciples shared their experiences with one another, a profound sense of unity and purpose emerged. They realized that love's essence, though deeply personal, was also a collective force—a universal energy that transcended individual boundaries and connected all souls.

Aurora, the guardian of the eternal flame, appeared before them, her presence radiating love's essence. She smiled, acknowledging the transformative journey the disciples had undertaken. Her voice, gentle and wise, filled the sanctuary.

"Beloved disciples, you have discovered a profound truth—the essence of love that resides within each and every one of you. Nurture this essence, for it is the key to unlocking the fullness of your potential as agents of love's transformative power."

She continued, her words resonating in their hearts, "As you continue your journey, remember that love's essence is boundless and eternal. It is the unifying force that transcends time and space, the catalyst for healing, growth, and unity. Embrace this essence within yourselves, and let it guide you as you illuminate the world with love's infinite radiance."

With a final embrace of love, Aurora dissolved into the eternal flame, leaving the disciples to bask in the profound realization of love's essence within. As they continued their journey, their souls ablaze with love's essence, they knew that they held within them the power to create a world where love reigned supreme. And with each step, they would shine their light, igniting the flame of love within all they encountered, for eternity.

Chapter 18 The Dance of Connection

In the realm of eternal love, the disciples found themselves drawn to the intricate dance of connection that wove through the fabric of existence. They recognized that love's essence, though residing within each being, yearned for the embrace of connection—a sacred union that transcended barriers and united souls in a symphony of love.

Guided by this understanding, the disciples set forth on a path of intentional connection. They ventured into realms both familiar and unknown, seeking opportunities to touch the lives of others and create meaningful bonds forged in the fires of love.

They journeyed through bustling cities, where hearts longed for authentic connection amid the cacophony of everyday life. With compassion in their eyes and love in their gestures, they offered a listening ear to those burdened by solitude and shared moments of genuine connection that reminded souls they were not alone.

In secluded villages, nestled amidst nature's embrace, the disciples encountered communities where love flourished in the simplicity of human connection. They joined in communal gatherings, dancing and singing with jubilant hearts, celebrating the unity that stemmed from shared experiences and collective expressions of love.

On their path, the disciples encountered souls yearning for connection yet apprehensive, their hearts guarded by past wounds. With patience and tenderness, the disciples extended a hand of understanding, encouraging these souls to peel back the layers of protection and trust in the transformative power of love.

In the presence of those who had forgotten their inherent worth, the disciples became mirrors of love, reflecting the beauty and brilliance that resided within. They reminded these souls of their unique gifts and their essential place in the tapestry of existence, igniting a spark of self-love and acceptance that radiated outward.

As the disciples deepened their connections, they discovered that true connection transcended superficial differences and embraced the essence of shared humanity. They saw the divinity in each being, recognizing that love knew no boundaries of race, gender, or belief. Love's essence was a unifying force that bridged the perceived divides, dissolving separation and weaving a tapestry of unity.

In their interactions, the disciples discovered the power of vulnerability—the sacred space where hearts met and souls intertwined. They courageously opened themselves to authentic expressions of their own joys, sorrows, fears, and hopes, inviting others to do the same. In these vulnerable exchanges, connections blossomed, and the dance of love grew ever more intricate.

The disciples gathered in a tranquil grove, their hearts filled with the resonance of connection. They sat in a circle, their eyes reflecting the love that flowed between them. Each disciple shared stories of the transformative connections they had forged, the lives they had touched, and the love that had blossomed.

Aurora, the guardian of the eternal flame, appeared before them, her presence a beacon of love's guidance. Her voice, imbued with wisdom and grace, filled the grove.

"Beloved disciples," she spoke, "in the dance of connection, you have discovered the power of love to bridge souls and weave a tapestry of unity. Embrace this dance, for it is through connection that you will find the true depth and beauty of love's essence."

She extended her hand, and as the disciples reached out, their hands interwove, creating a radiant web of connection. Aurora continued, "Together, you form a constellation of love, united in your commitment to forge connections that transcend time and space. Continue to dance this sacred dance, touching lives and inspiring hearts with the transformative power of love."

With gratitude in their hearts, the disciples acknowledged their interconnectedness and vowed to nurture the dance of connection within themselves and in the world around them. They understood that love's essence shone brightest when it flowed through the channels of connection, weaving a tapestry of unity that echoed throughout eternity.

And so, with hearts intertwined and love as their guide, the disciples set forth once again, ready to embark on the next chapter of their journey—a chapter that would unfold with the grace of connection and the boundless potential of love's eternal dance.

Chapter 19 The Awakening of Compassion

In the realm of eternal love, a gentle breeze whispered through the hearts of the disciples, carrying with it a call to awaken the dormant power of compassion. They understood that love's essence, when coupled with compassion, had the ability to heal wounds, soothe pain, and ignite transformation in the lives of all beings.

Inspired by this call, the disciples set out on a path that would deepen their understanding of compassion and its profound impact on the world. They ventured into realms where suffering thrived, where hearts longed for solace and kindness amid the trials of existence.

In the bustling cities, they encountered individuals burdened by the weight of their own struggles, their souls yearning for compassion amidst the chaos. The disciples offered a compassionate ear, listening deeply to the stories that unfolded before them. With open hearts and empathetic understanding, they extended love's embrace, providing solace and reminding these souls that they were seen, heard, and cherished.

In remote villages, the disciples witnessed the plight of those marginalized and forgotten by society. With humility and determination, they rolled up their sleeves and immersed themselves in acts of service. They built shelters, tended to the sick, and nourished hungry bellies. Through their acts of compassion, they restored dignity and kindled hope in the hearts of those they touched.

The disciples encountered souls who had closed themselves off from the world, their pain and fear becoming barriers to receiving love. With gentle persistence, they cultivated patience and understanding, nurturing trust in the hearts of these souls. They showed them that compassion was not only about giving but also about receiving the healing balm of love from others.

In their own moments of vulnerability, the disciples discovered that compassion was not limited to external acts, but a deep wellspring that resided within. They learned to offer themselves the same tender compassion they extended to others, embracing their own wounds and insecurities with love's gentle touch. By tending to their own hearts, they discovered that their capacity for compassion grew exponentially.

As the disciples delved deeper into the realms of suffering, they encountered the dark corners of their own souls—the moments of judgment, indifference, and apathy. With unwavering commitment to growth, they acknowledged these aspects within themselves, choosing to transform them with the radiant light of compassion.

They recognized that compassion was not confined to individual acts, but a collective force that could bring about systemic change. They joined forces with organizations and advocates dedicated to addressing social injustice and alleviating the suffering of the marginalized. Through their collective efforts, they ignited a wave of compassion that rippled through communities and instigated positive transformation.

In a serene sanctuary within the realm, the disciples gathered to reflect on their journey of compassion. They sat in a circle, their eyes reflecting the depth of their experiences. Each disciple shared stories of the lives touched, the compassion received, and the transformation witnessed.

Aurora, the guardian of the eternal flame, materialized before them, her presence radiating compassion's gentle warmth. Her voice, filled with love's tender grace, enveloped the sanctuary.

"Beloved disciples," she spoke, "in awakening the power of compassion, you have touched lives, healed wounds, and ignited the flames of transformation. Embrace this sacred gift, for it is through compassion that love's essence finds its fullest expression."

She extended her hands, and as the disciples reached out, their hands intertwined in a circle of compassion. Aurora continued, "Together, you are beacons of compassion, bringing light to the darkest corners of existence. Let your compassion guide you, for in the dance of compassion, you will witness the true beauty of love's essence."

With hearts overflowing with gratitude, the disciples acknowledged the interconnectedness of compassion and love. They vowed to carry the torch of compassion with unwavering devotion, knowing that their acts of kindness and understanding would continue to sow seeds of love's transformative power.

And so, with their hearts aglow with compassion, the disciples ventured forth once again, ready to embark on the next chapter of their journey—a chapter that would unfold with the profound impact of compassion and the unwavering commitment to the well-being of all beings.

Chapter 20 The Eternal Legacy of Love

In the realm of eternal love, the disciples stood at the threshold of the final chapter of their remarkable journey. The tapestry of their experiences was woven with threads of love, connection, compassion, and transformation. Now, they found themselves on the precipice of a profound realization—a realization that would shape their eternal legacy.

With hearts brimming with gratitude and wisdom, the disciples gathered in a sacred grove, surrounded by the beauty of nature. They shared stories of their individual growth, the lives touched, and the countless miracles witnessed. Each tale illuminated the transformative power of love's essence and the ripple effect it created throughout the cosmos.

As the disciples reflected upon their collective journey, they understood that the time had come to distill the essence of their experiences into a legacy that would resonate for eternity. They engaged in deep contemplation, seeking to understand the unique contribution they were called to make.

In the stillness of the grove, a gentle breeze whispered through the trees, carrying with it the voices of the souls they had touched. The chorus of gratitude and love stirred their spirits, guiding them toward a profound realization— their eternal legacy would be one of inspiration and empowerment.

With renewed purpose, the disciples embarked on a mission to inspire others to embrace the fullness of their own divine potential. They became mentors and guides, sharing their wisdom and experiences with those who sought the path of love. Through their words and actions, they ignited sparks of hope, courage, and self-discovery, empowering others to embark on their own transformative journeys.

The disciples recognized that their legacy would not be limited to their physical presence in the realm of eternal love. They were called to extend their reach beyond the boundaries of time and space, weaving their legacy into the very fabric of existence.

They harnessed the power of storytelling, weaving tales of love, connection, compassion, and transformation. Their stories would traverse dimensions, touching the hearts and souls of beings across the vast cosmos. Through these narratives, they would perpetuate the eternal flame of love, inspiring generations to come.

In their interactions with others, the disciples became living embodiments of love's essence. They radiated authenticity, kindness, and understanding, leaving an indelible imprint on the hearts of those they encountered. They understood that even the simplest acts of love held the potential to ripple outward, influencing the course of countless lives.

As the final pages of their journey unfolded, the disciples came to understand that their legacy was not defined by grand gestures or monumental achievements, but by the small, meaningful moments of love and connection they had cultivated. They realized that true legacy lay in the hearts they had touched, the lives they had transformed, and the eternal flame of love they had kindled within each soul.

In a final gathering, the disciples stood before the eternal flame, its radiant glow a testament to the love they had nurtured. Aurora, the guardian of the flame, stood beside them, her presence a beacon of guidance and love.

"Beloved disciples," Aurora spoke, her voice carrying the wisdom of eternity, "you have journeyed through the realms of love, connection, compassion, and transformation. In this final chapter, you have discovered the true essence of your legacy—to inspire and empower others to embrace the boundless power of love."

She extended her hand, and as the disciples reached out, their hands formed a circle, symbolizing the eternal nature of their bond. Aurora continued, "As you step into the vast expanse of eternity, carry with you the lessons and experiences of your journey. Let your legacy be one of love's infinite potential, igniting hearts and awakening souls to the profound truth that love is the essence of all existence."

With tears of joy and hearts full of love, the disciples embraced the truth of their eternal legacy. They vowed to continue their journey in realms yet unexplored, carrying the flame of love within their beings and forever inspiring the universe with their luminous presence.

And so, as the final chapter came to a close, the disciples stepped forward, their spirits aflame with love, connection, compassion, and transformation. They vanished into the ether, their legacy woven into the very fabric of existence, forever shaping the destiny of the cosmos with the eternal essence of love.